TITANIC

Anna Claybourne and Katie Daynes

Designed by Katarina Dragoslavic

Illustrations by Ian McNee

Ship consultant: David Livingstone,
retired naval architect, Harland and Wolff Ltd.

SCHOLASTIC INC.

New York   Toronto   London   Auckland   Sydney
Mexico City   New Delhi   Hong Kong   Buenos Aires

ISBN-13: 978-0-439-93257-8
ISBN-10: 0-439-93257-2

12 11 10 9 8   9 10 11 12/0

Printed in the U.S.A.   23

First Scholastic printing, March 2007

Reading consultant: Alison Kelly, Roehampton University

Series editor: Jane Chisholm

Cover designed by Russell Punter and illustrated by Sergio

CONTENTS

NORTH
AMERICA

NEWFOUNDLAND

NOVA SCOTIA

New York

ATLANTIC OCEAN

THE TITANIC'S
SCHEDULED JOURNEY

GREENLAND

Belfast

IRELAND

BRITAIN

Queenstown

Southampton

Cherbourg

FRANCE

CHAPTER 1
THE "UNSINKABLE" SHIP

In the early 1900s, there were no passenger
planes. If you wanted to cross a vast ocean,
you had to go by sea. Two rival companies
running fleets of ships were the Cunard Line
and the White Star Line. Both carried mail
and passengers between America and Europe.
When Cunard introduced two fast new
ships, White Star was determined not to
be outdone.

Bruce Ismay, the White Star boss, commissioned three huge liners with names to reflect their size – *Olympic, Titanic* and *Gigantic.* Like the new Cunard ships, they would be powered by steam, but they would be 50% bigger and twice as luxurious. From the start, the emphasis was on comfort and safety, not speed.

"Our ships will be the largest, most elegant liners afloat," announced Ismay. "And we'll have people lining up to buy tickets!"

White Star employed the shipbuilders Harland and Wolff for the job. They owned an enormous shipyard in Belfast, Ireland. In December 1908, they began construction work on the *Olympic.* Three months later, on the adjacent slipway, the framework for the *Titanic* was laid out.

Over the next two years, thousands of workers scurried around the shipyard, climbing scaffolding, operating cranes and

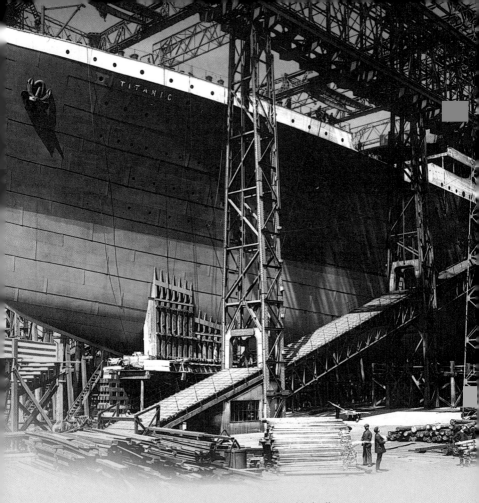

Here you can see the *Titanic*'s hull near completion in the Harland and Wolff shipyard.

fitting parts. No expense was spared and gradually the *Olympic*, then the *Titanic*, towered over the other ships.

Their eight decks each reached as high as a 17-floor tower block and from stern to bow they were the length of 40 buses. The ships' steel hulls were 2.5 to 5cm (1 to 2 inches) thick. For safety reasons, they were divided into 16 separate compartments. The ships would still stay afloat even if a massive hole was gouged in the side and two of the compartments were flooded. According to *The Shipbuilder* magazine, the *Olympic* and *Titanic* were practically unsinkable.

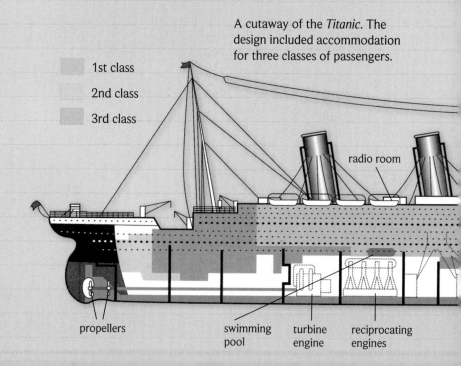

A cutaway of the *Titanic*. The design included accommodation for three classes of passengers.

1st class
2nd class
3rd class

radio room

propellers

swimming pool

turbine engine

reciprocating engines

The White Star Line's New Triple-screw Steamers
"OLYMPIC" ☆ "TITANIC"
LARGEST AND FINEST IN THE WORLD

This White Star poster shows that their new steamers, if balanced on their end, would tower above the tallest skyscraper in America.

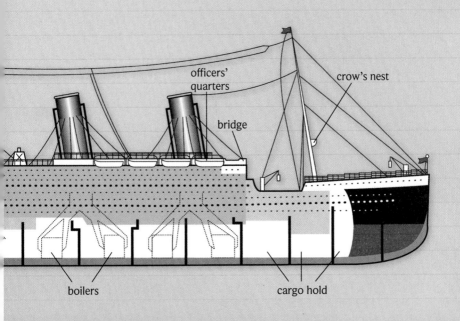

officers' quarters

crow's nest

bridge

boilers

cargo hold

The *Olympic* was launched with great fanfare on October 20th, 1910. It hit the headlines as the biggest ship ever to ride the waves. Seven months later, the *Titanic* was ready to enter the water, too.

By now, White Star's ships were famous. Over 100,000 people gathered to witness the launch. A red flag was raised on the stern and a red rocket was fired into the sky, warning other boats to keep their distance.

At 12:13pm, the gigantic hull was released and slid down the slipway.

"There she goes!" cried the workers, watching the ship glide gracefully into the water. A minute later, the *Titanic* was afloat.

It would take another year to transform the ship from an empty hull into a five-star floating hotel, but already its size and shape had captured the imaginations of many.

On May 31st, 1911, the *Titanic* entered the water for the first time.

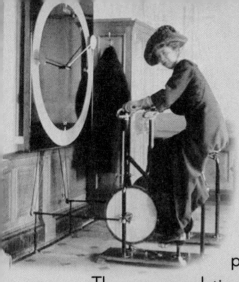

This passenger is trying out an exercise bike in the *Titanic*'s gym.

On board there would be a gym, a swimming pool, tennis courts, a library... and even kennels for the passengers' dogs.

The accommodation was designed for three classes of passengers: luxurious suites for first class, comfortable rooms for second class and basic cabins with bunkbeds for third class.

A first-class suite on board the *Titanic*. Its furnishings and decor were seen as the height of luxury in 1912.

Deep down in the hull were 29 massive coal-fired boilers. They belted out steam to power the engines, which in turn made the three huge propellers rotate in the water.

Companies were eager to supply items for the *Titanic*, from doors and sofas to stationery and soap. They thought it wonderful to be associated with such a glamorous ship.

In this advertisement a company uses the *Titanic* to promote its soap.

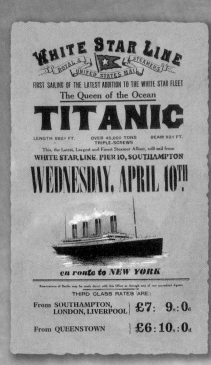

White Star printed large posters with details of the *Titanic*'s first voyage.

Meanwhile people rushed to buy their tickets. On April 10th, 1912, the *Titanic* would leave Southampton docks in England for New York, USA.

22-year-old Alice Cleaver couldn't believe her luck. Her employers, the Allisons, had bought her a first-class ticket. They were a very wealthy family, returning via New York to their home in Canada, and they wanted Alice to come too, as a nanny for their baby son, Trevor.

Hungarian stone carver, Leopold Weisz, bought two second-class tickets. He had saved up a small fortune, so he and his wife,

Mathilde, could start a new life overseas.

The Quicks also had second-class tickets. Eight-year-old Winifred Quick was off to join her dad in New York, along with her mother and her sister, Phyllis.

Poorer passengers had to sell everything they owned to buy a third-class, one-way ticket to America. They hoped it would lead to a better life. Among them were Wilhelm Skoog, his wife, Anna, and their four children.

Altogether, 1,316 people bought tickets, but there would be many more on board. Captain Edward John Smith was in charge of the *Titanic*'s vast crew of over 900 workers. They included officers, seamen, radio operators, engineers, waiters, musicians and dozens of firemen who had the hot, dusty job of keeping the boiler fires burning around the clock.

Captain
E.J. Smith

15

On April 2nd, the *Titanic* left Belfast to undergo sea trials. Tugs towed the liner into open water, then cast off. Slowly, the huge propellers began to revolve. For the first time, the *Titanic* was moving under its own steam. All day, the ship stopped and started, churned around in circles and snaked through the water at various speeds. It easily completed the sea trials and was allowed to sail on to Southampton docks.

The final days of preparation were frantic. The *Titanic* had to be stocked with everything from bedding and tableware to food and drink. And still there were workmen on board fitting carpets and hanging curtains.

Meanwhile, a steady stream of trucks, horses and carts unloaded hundreds more cases to be transported in the ship's hold. They contained items ranging from ribbons to toothpaste, all destined for various American companies.

Tug boats towed the *Titanic* from Belfast to the open sea, where the steamship would undergo its sea trials.

CHAPTER 2
THE MAIDEN VOYAGE

On April 10th, expectant crowds gathered to witness the *Titanic*'s departure. Passengers flooded up the gangway, some accompanied by family or friends who wanted to see inside the magnificent steamship. Then, just after noon, three loud whistles blew out. People without tickets said quick farewells and hurried back to the quay as the *Titanic* prepared to leave.

Five tug boats began their heavy work, pulling the steamship out into the river. Suddenly, there was a loud cry from the quay. "Wait for us!" Eight crew members were racing to the ship. They had stayed for one too many drinks in the pub.

Two of them managed to reach the gangway on time, but the others had missed their chance. They watched, frustrated, as the mighty liner moved out of reach.

Once the tugs were safely away from the shore, they dropped their tow lines and the *Titanic* was all alone. Then the gigantic propellers began to rotate once more, driving the ship on through the waves.

Excited passengers crowded the deck as the *Titanic* left the port.

But as the *Titanic* surged past another ship – the *New York* – there was a sound like gunshot. The *New York*'s mooring ropes had snapped. Now it was swinging towards the *Titanic*, as if pulled by a giant magnet.

The passengers watched in horror, fearing a collision. Luckily, Captain Smith's quick instructions steered the *Titanic* away and they continued along Southampton's broad river to the open sea beyond.

The *Titanic*'s first two stops were Cherbourg in France and Queenstown in southern Ireland. A few passengers left and more climbed aboard.

At Queenstown, one of the firemen, John Coffey, deserted the ship. He hid under some sacks on a mailboat and got a lift to shore. No one knows why. He might have signed up to work on the *Titanic* simply to get a free trip home. Or maybe Coffey was worried about the voyage and wanted to escape.

The *Titanic* was too large
to dock at Queenstown,
so mailboats ferried
passengers to the ship,
then collected any mail.

There were certainly some people who felt afraid. From Queenstown, the chief officer Henry Wilde sent a worried letter to his sister. "I still don't like this ship," he wrote. "I have a queer feeling about it."

Journalist William Thomas Stead was concerned too. He had been plagued with visions of shipwrecks and, recently, a fortune-teller had warned him to avoid ocean crossings. But the American President had asked him to speak at a peace conference. It was an invitation Stead couldn't refuse.

In total, 55 people cancelled their bookings on the *Titanic*. Some were nervous about making a maiden journey; others cancelled for health or business reasons. But most passengers just reasoned that nothing could harm such a huge ship. They only had to look at the *Olympic*'s successful journeys for reassurance.

The *Titanic* left Queenstown on April 11th and glided out across the Atlantic Ocean, heading for New York. If all went according to plan, the journey would take six days.

The *Titanic* continued its journey across the vast Atlantic Ocean.

Passengers braved the brisk weather on deck.

For two days, everything went perfectly. The weather was chilly but fine and the sea was very calm. During the day, people chatted in the lounges, relaxed in the reading rooms and went for walks on deck. Each evening, the first-class passengers dressed in their finest clothes to dine, while the Skoogs and others in steerage told stories, danced jigs and sang folk songs.

Captain Smith was pleased with the ship's progress. By lunchtime on the third day, they had covered over 2,300km (1,400 miles). They were already halfway through their journey, and he predicted the *Titanic* would reach New York early on Wednesday, April 17th.

By now, the ship was in the North Atlantic Ocean, about 650km (400 miles) from Newfoundland, Canada. For several days, other ships had been radioing messages to the *Titanic*, warning the crew of icebergs ahead.

This map illustrates the *Titanic*'s location on the third day.

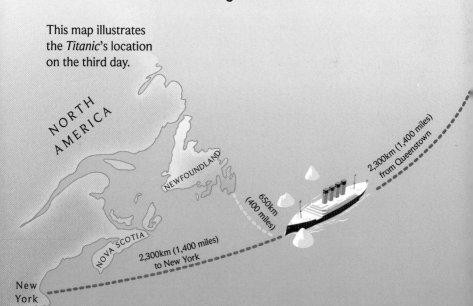

The iceberg threat

Icebergs are floating chunks
of ice that have broken off
from glaciers.

Most of an iceberg is
underwater, hidden from view.
The ice is rock-hard. For a ship, hitting
an iceberg is as bad as hitting rocks.

As night fell on Sunday, April 14th, two
lookouts, Frederick Fleet and Reginald Lee,
took their places in the crow's nest to keep
watch for icebergs. It was a difficult job.
Shivering in the bitter cold, they peered
into the darkness, searching for signs of ice.
Meanwhile, the *Titanic* steamed ahead at
full speed.

CHAPTER 3

ICEBERG!

An hour and a half went by, and the watchmen grew colder. They were looking forward to snuggling down in their warm bunks. Then, at 11:40pm, Frederick Fleet saw an ominous object loom out of the ocean. It could only be one thing. He telephoned the bridge, where the ship's officers were on duty. "Iceberg, right ahead!" he cried.

An iceberg can be harder to spot in a calm sea because there are no splashes of water at the edges.

First officer William Murdoch acted fast. He ordered the crew to shut down the engines and steer the ship hard to port (to the left). But a ship as big as the *Titanic* takes a long time to change direction. 30 seconds ticked by, and the lookouts watched in panic as they neared the threatening iceberg.

Then, at the last moment, the *Titanic* turned. Instead of hitting the iceberg head-on, the ship scraped along the side of it. Chunks of ice broke off and fell onto the deck.

This illustration shows how the *Titanic* scraped along the side of the iceberg.

Underwater, the iceberg gouged holes through the *Titanic*'s metal hull.

The collision was so gentle, the passengers felt nothing but a slight bump. Some of them were still up, having a drink after dinner. Many were in their nightclothes. Hundreds of third-class passengers, like the Skoog children, were fast asleep in their bunks on the lower decks. They didn't even wake up.

But Captain Smith, resting in his cabin, felt a jolt and hurried up to the bridge. "What have we struck?" he asked his first officer, urgently.

"An iceberg, sir," replied Murdoch.

"Have you closed the watertight doors?"

"They are already closed, sir."

As messages from different parts of the ship came through, Smith realized the *Titanic* was in big trouble. By dragging along the ship's side, the iceberg had ripped several holes in a row along the hull. Now, ice-cold water was flooding the cargo and boiler rooms.

Smith knew the ship was safe as long as only two compartments were flooded. But water was already pouring into five. The *Titanic* was going to sink.

A diagram showing water in five of the *Titanic*'s compartments

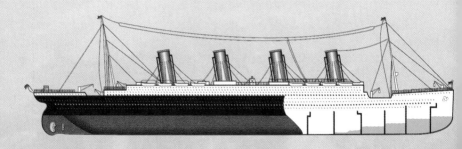

Captain Smith summoned Thomas Andrews, the ship's designer. "How long have we got?" he asked.

Andrews did some quick calculations. "Only two hours, sir," he announced.

Captain Smith ordered the crew to wake the passengers, give them lifejackets, fire off distress flares and prepare the lifeboats.

Radio operator John Phillips sent out a distress call. He gave the ship's position and a CQD, meaning "Come Quick – Danger!"

There were several ships nearby, but it was midnight and most radio operators had finished work and gone to bed. By chance, Harold Cottam on board the Cunard liner *Carpathia* chose that moment to forward a message to the *Titanic*. "Come at once," replied Phillips. "We have struck an iceberg."

Cottam burst into his captain's cabin and, within minutes, the *Carpathia* was steaming towards the *Titanic*. But, even at full speed, it was at least a three-hour journey.

This photo shows a radio operator on board the *Titanic*.

The *Titanic*'s lifeboats

Back on the *Titanic*, the crew uncovered the lifeboats. Unfortunately, there were only 20. The designers had believed the great liner was so sturdy, it could act as its own lifeboat. They never dreamed it might sink. There were only enough lifeboats for 1,200 people, but over 2,200 needed to be rescued.

Officers asked women and children to board the boats first, but hardly any of them wanted to. The *Titanic* was still steady on the water and people couldn't believe it was really sinking. Some continued playing cards or drinking. Others played football with broken chunks of ice on deck.

When the women and children hesitated, a few anxious men climbed in. Then the first few lifeboats, still only half full, were lowered onto the sea.

An hour later, the ship was at a definite slant. Chairs and tables slowly slid across the deck and people began to panic. As more flares rocketed into the sky, passengers dashed for the few remaining lifeboats.

This is the last message ever sent from the *Titanic*.

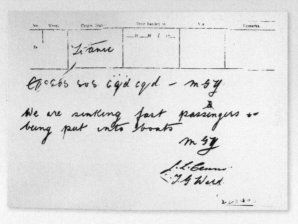

Meanwhile, the brave band members kept playing jazz. They hoped it would keep people's spirits up.

Now the problem on the lifeboats was overcrowding. One officer had to fire his pistol to stop extra people from jumping on.

Alice Cleaver, the Allisons' nanny, grabbed baby Trevor and took a place in lifeboat 11. Trevor's mother found herself in a different lifeboat with her daughter, Loraine. She was

A scene from the film *Titanic* shows the panic as people clamber onto lifeboats.

desperate to find the rest of her family, so she dragged Loraine back onto the ship... and missed their chance to escape.

Winifred Quick was also in boat 11, stowed safely with her family. Since only women and children were allowed at first, Mathilde Weisz had to leave her beloved husband Leopold on the *Titanic*. She climbed into lifeboat 10, heartbroken and in tears.

People in first class were nearer to the lifeboats and most likely to escape. As for the Skoog family, and many others in third class, they were stuck on board. Bruce Ismay got a place in one of the last lifeboats. But E.J. Smith knew a captain should never desert his ship. He stayed on deck with hundreds of other men and watched, helpless, as the lifeboats rowed away. All these men could do was wait for the ship to sink, with only their lifejackets to save them.

CHAPTER 4

GOING DOWN...

By two in the morning, the front of the *Titanic* had tilted forward so much, waves were lapping over the bow. There was a huge clattering inside. Everything — furniture, candlesticks, silverware, glasses — tumbled forward. Everybody on deck clambered up to the stern, grabbed the railings and hung on for their lives.

A roaring, noise ripped through the night, as the *Titanic's* steel hull began to tear apart.

650 km (400 miles)

The front half disappeared underwater, while the back half tilted right up into the air. Those watching from the lifeboats saw the stern tower above the water, still lit from within, and heard the cries of men left dangling from the railings or slipping to their deaths.

Then, after a dramatic pause, the vast ocean liner plunged straight down. The lights flickered and went out as the ship was swallowed by the sea. Deeper and deeper it sank through the dark water, finally coming to rest on the sea bed, almost 4km (2½ miles) below the surface.

4 km (2.5 miles)

The *Titanic*'s resting place

One survivor, John B. Thayer, sketched his impression of how the
Titanic sank. Experts who have studied the disaster think some of
Thayer's details are inaccurate.

STRIKES STARBOARD BOW - 12.1 AM.   11 ⁴⁵ P.M.

SETTLES BY HEAD - BOATS ORDERED OUT   12 ⁰⁵ AM

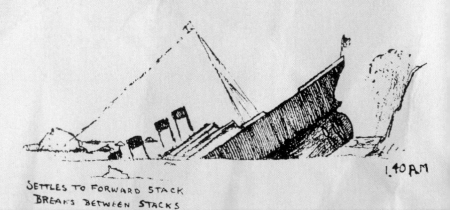

1.40 AM

SETTLES TO FORWARD STACK
BREAKS BETWEEN STACKS

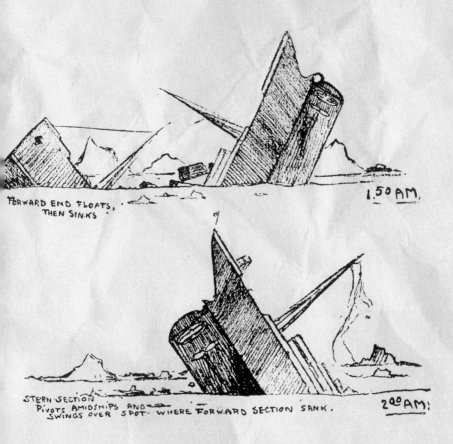

FORWARD END FLOATS,
THEN SINKS

1.50 AM.

STERN SECTION
PIVOTS AMIDSHIPS AND
SWINGS OVER SPOT WHERE FORWARD SECTION SANK.

2.00 AM.

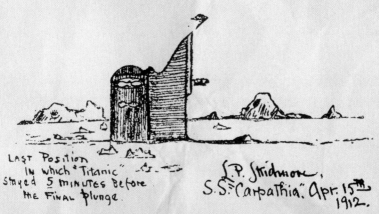

LAST POSITION
IN WHICH "TITANIC"
STAYED 5 MINUTES BEFORE
THE FINAL PLUNGE.

J.P. Skidmore,
S.S. "Carpathia" Apr. 15TH
1912.

People on board were either dragged under with the ship or tossed into the icy water. Thanks to their lifejackets, many stayed afloat. But the water was so cold, it was impossible to stay alive for long.

The sea was 28°F (-2°C) — colder than freezing. It hadn't frozen solid, because salty water freezes at a lower temperature than fresh water. But floating in it was like being encased in a block of ice. At those temperatures, most people can't survive for longer than half an hour. And the *Carpathia* was still an hour away.

The people in the lifeboats had quickly rowed away from the *Titanic*, so they didn't get sucked under as the ship sank. Now they were faced with an awful decision. There were still empty seats in some of the boats, but nowhere near enough for the hundreds of people who needed rescuing. If the lifeboats returned, they would risk being swamped and sunk by desperate people clambering aboard.

So the lifeboats stayed where they were, their passengers paralyzed by shock and sadness. Across the waves came screams and groans, each one weaker than the last.

Most of the survivors in this lifeboat were women and children.

In the end, only one boat — containing *Titanic* crew members — went back to the scene. A few people were found alive and pulled to safety, but most of the bodies in the water were dead.

Out of more than 2,200 passengers, just 705 survived. They shivered in the freezing cold and huddled together in the lifeboats, traumatized by the night's events and worried for their loved ones.

Far on the horizon, they saw the lights of another ship. But it sailed on by. It hadn't seen the *Titanic*'s distress flares, or heard the radio messages. Only the *Carpathia* could save them.

These passengers had to wait two hours in their lifeboat before they were rescued.

This diagram shows other ships'
positions on the night of the disaster,
and their distances from the *Titanic*.

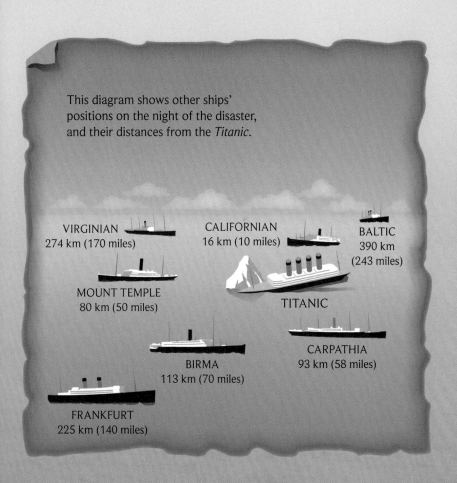

VIRGINIAN
274 km (170 miles)

CALIFORNIAN
16 km (10 miles)

BALTIC
390 km
(243 miles)

MOUNT TEMPLE
80 km (50 miles)

TITANIC

CARPATHIA
93 km (58 miles)

BIRMA
113 km (70 miles)

FRANKFURT
225 km (140 miles)

The captain of the *Carpathia*, Arthur
Rostron, was doing everything he could. He
ordered his crew to set up first-aid rooms and
prepare the lifeboats. "Drink lots of coffee,"
he told them. "It's going to be a long night."

Captain Rostron

Soon there were blankets, hot soup, tea and brandy waiting for the survivors. Incredulous whispers spread through the cabins. "But they said the *Titanic* was unsinkable!"

Captain Rostron switched off the heating so every bit of steam from the boilers could be used to power the engines. Although the sea was strewn with icebergs, Rostron's crew raced on through the night, to the site of the disaster.

Some of the icebergs in the Atlantic are much bigger than a steamship.

The *Carpathia*

CHAPTER 5

CARPATHIA TO THE RESCUE

At last, at 3:30am, over an hour after the *Titanic* had gone down, the *Carpathia* arrived. To Captain Rostron's dismay, there was no sign of the ship. All he could see was darkness.

The survivors saw rockets being fired from the *Carpathia* and knew someone had come to help them. They jumped up and waved their arms. But another 40 minutes went by before the *Carpathia*'s crew spotted the tiny lifeboats on the inky black water.

At 4:10am, lifeboat 2 pulled
alongside the *Carpathia* and the
survivors began to climb onto the
ship. The first aboard was a
first-class passenger,
29-year-old Elizabeth
Allen. She quickly
described what
had happened.

This photo shows one of the
Titanic's lifeboats reaching
the safety of the *Carpathia*.

Over the next few hours, all 705 survivors were taken aboard the *Carpathia*. Those who were strong enough climbed up a rope ladder onto the ship. Sacks and cargo nets were lowered over the side, so children and less agile people could be pulled up on deck. Then they were rushed to the first-aid rooms, where frostbite, cuts and broken bones were seen to.

The survivors' relief at being rescued was mixed with panic and sorrow. They prayed their loved ones had made it onto another lifeboat and searched desperately for them. But most searched in vain.

As the sun rose, Captain Rostron scoured the hostile sea. It was soon clear that there was no one else to save. He ordered the *Carpathia*'s flag to be lowered to half mast and organized a memorial service as they passed over the place where the *Titanic* had gone down.

Just then, another ship — the *Californian* — arrived to help. But there was nothing more to do. The *Carpathia* had been sailing east, from New York to Gibraltar. Now Rostron decided they should head west, back to New York. The survivors had already been through so much, taking them straight to their destination seemed the kindest thing to do.

It would take the *Carpathia* three days to reach New York. Meanwhile, the world was eager to hear about the *Titanic*'s progress. Radio operator, Harold Cottam, had to break the awful news.

In London, the *Evening News* was quick to report the disaster.

TITANIC
DISASTER
GREAT LOSS
OF LIFE
EVENING NEWS

The New York Times.

VOL. LXI...NO. 19,806.   NEW YORK, TUESDAY, APRIL 16, 1912.—TWENTY-FOUR PAGES.   ONE CENT

TITANIC SINKS FOUR HOURS AFTER HITTING ICEBERG; 866 RESCUED BY CARPATHIA, PROBABLY 1250 PERISH; ISMAY SAFE, MRS. ASTOR MAYBE, NOTED NAMES MISSING

Col. Astor and Bride, Isidor Straus and Wife, and Maj. Butt Aboard.

"RULE OF SEA" FOLLOWED

Women and Children Put Over in Lifeboats and Are Supposed to be Safe on Carpathia.

PICKED UP AFTER 8 HOURS

Vincent Astor Calls at White Star Office for News of His Father and Leaves Weeping.

FRANKLIN HOPEFUL ALL DAY

Manager of the Line Insisted Titanic Was Unsinkable Even After She Had Gone Down.

HEAD OF THE LINE ABOARD

Biggest Liner Plunges to the Bottom at 2:20 A.M.

RESCUERS THERE TOO LATE

Except to Pick Up the Few Hundreds Who Took to the Lifeboats.

WOMEN AND CHILDREN FIRST

Camrose Carpathia Rushing to New York with the Survivors.

SEA SEARCH FOR OTHERS

The California Stands By on Chance of Picking Up Other Boats or Rafts.

OLYMPIC SENDS THE NEWS

Only Ship to Flash Wireless Messages to Shore After the Disaster.

The Lost Titanic Being Towed Out of Belfast Harbor.

PARTIAL LIST OF THE SAVED.

The sinking of the *Titanic* made front page news in *The New York Times* on April 14th, 1912.

Long before the ship reached port, newspapers on both sides of the Atlantic were reporting the disaster. The news became garbled as it was passed on and many of the accounts were full of mistakes. Some newspapers said the *Titanic* had sunk, but no one had been hurt, while others said the *Titanic* was still afloat and being towed to safety.

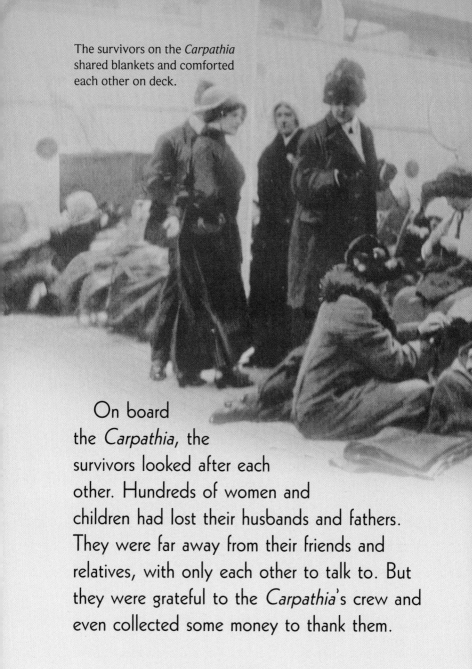

The survivors on the *Carpathia* shared blankets and comforted each other on deck.

On board the *Carpathia*, the survivors looked after each other. Hundreds of women and children had lost their husbands and fathers. They were far away from their friends and relatives, with only each other to talk to. But they were grateful to the *Carpathia*'s crew and even collected some money to thank them.

Mathilde Weisz tried to keep busy. It distracted her from thinking of her poor husband, Leopold. It was her brainwave to take napkins from the *Carpathia*'s dining rooms and use them as nappies or diapers for the babies.

On the evening of Thursday, April 18th, the *Carpathia* arrived in New York. The weather was stormy and lightning flashed across the dark sky as the ship entered the docks.

Thousands of people waited in the misty rain, including government representatives and hordes of journalists, but only close relatives were allowed on the pier. A respectful silence greeted the ship, followed by tears of joy when the first survivors appeared.

Passengers on the *Carpathia* would have seen the city of New York looming through the storm clouds.

Doctors and nurses stood by, ready to treat the injured and take them to a hospital. At every turn, reporters shouted questions and flashed cameras. They were desperate to capture the whole shocking story.

Survivors such as the Quicks experienced a happy ending as they were reunited with their families. Winifred Quick later married and had five children. She died in 2002, aged 98.

Others, like Alice Cleaver, found themselves in a strange city with nowhere to go. Alice soon went back to England. Trevor Allison, the baby she had saved, was adopted by his aunt and uncle and grew up in Canada.

Mathilde Weisz stepped off the ship, alone and penniless. Later, her husband's body was found floating in the Atlantic, his fortune sewn safely into his suit. With the money, Mathilde set up a home for herself in Canada.

The *Titanic*'s crew were the last to leave the *Carpathia*. They were taken to another ship, heading straight back to England.

Here, experts and witnesses tried to establish why the *Titanic* sank.

The *Titanic* disaster forced the world to realize that no ship, however powerful and well-designed, was unsinkable. In Britain and America there were inquiries to find out why so many people — more than 1,500 altogether — had lost their lives.

As a result, new laws were passed to make sure such a disaster could never happen again. Ice patrols were introduced, all ships were ordered to carry enough lifeboats to seat all their passengers, and a radio operator had to be on duty in each ship 24 hours a day.

CHAPTER 6
THE *TITANIC* LIVES ON

The sinking of the *Titanic* is one of the world's most memorable disasters. Ever since, people have been interviewing the survivors and writing books about the fateful journey. Many films have tried to recreate the horror and heroism of that night, as well as the luxury and magnificence of the ship.

This film scene shows passengers on the *Titanic*'s first-class promenade deck.

One of the earliest *Titanic* films is called *A Night to Remember*. Made in 1958, it was based on a book about the disaster by Walter Lord. It told the story of the ship and passengers as truthfully as possible.

Other films, such as the 1997 blockbuster *Titanic*, added fictional characters and romanticized the story. *Titanic* broke box office records — proof that the story of the "unsinkable" ship still fascinates people today.

The *Titanic* film crew used a model of the ship for some of their scenes.

As for the *Titanic*, this once great liner remains on the ocean floor, at the very bottom of the north Atlantic. Some of the rich survivors hoped to raise the ship to the surface. They were prepared to pay vast amounts of money for the project. But, before the 1920s, no one knew how to find the wreck, let alone lift it from the sea bed.

As technology improved during the 20th century, there were many search attempts. Most used a method called sonar. Sonar works by sending sound waves down to the sea bed, then collecting the echoes as they bounce back. It can often detect unusual shapes, such as shipwrecks. But the sonar searches couldn't find the *Titanic*.

This diagram shows sound waves detecting a whale underwater.

Then in 1985, an American scientist, Dr. Robert Ballard, tried a new method. He had invented an underwater device called *Argo*. It could dive to the sea bed, take pictures, and send them back to a ship on the surface. A little robot, named *Jason*, was attached to *Argo*. It could move in and take closer pictures.

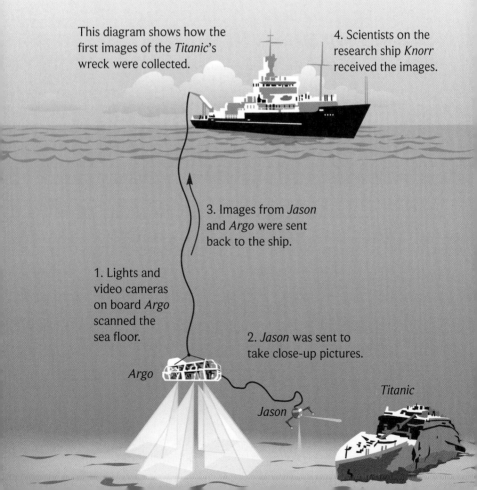

This diagram shows how the first images of the *Titanic*'s wreck were collected.

4. Scientists on the research ship *Knorr* received the images.

3. Images from *Jason* and *Argo* were sent back to the ship.

1. Lights and video cameras on board *Argo* scanned the sea floor.

2. *Jason* was sent to take close-up pictures.

Argo

Jason

Titanic

Ballard and his team sailed to the area where the *Titanic* had sunk, and sent the *Argo* down. After 10 days of searching, they saw pictures of debris scattered across the ocean floor, including a huge boiler. At last, the wreck of the *Titanic* had been found.

A submersible hovering over the wreck of the *Titanic*

Over the next few years, Ballard and other scientists explored the skeleton of the ship inside mini-submarines called submersibles or subs. They floated around the *Titanic*'s ghostly hull, taking photos and peering in at portholes. They also picked up objects from the wreck using robot arms attached to their subs.

For the first time, the world could see pictures of the *Titanic* as it lay in pieces on the sea bed. Museums put on exhibitions displaying everyday items used on board. Some were collected from the sea floor, others donated by survivors and their families.

Tickets, watches, cutlery, playing cards, teacups and clothes all gave clues to what life had been like on the ill-fated liner. Crowds flocked to see them and interest in the *Titanic* grew stronger than ever.

This bag belonged to one of the *Titanic*'s officers. It was retrieved from the wreck of the *Titanic*.

The Big Piece — a section of the *Titanic*'s hull — was raised to the surface in 1998.

In 1996, a team of French scientists tried to raise a large section of the *Titanic*'s broken hull, known as the Big Piece. The first attempt went wrong. The cables holding the Big Piece snapped and it fell back onto the sea bed.

Two years later, the scientists finally managed to get it onto dry land. Since then, millions of people have been to see it.

Some people still dream of raising the rest of the *Titanic* from the sea bed. But the ship is so huge, it would be virtually impossible. For now, the famous steamship lies in a watery grave, far beneath the waves, at the bottom of the Atlantic Ocean.

TITANIC TIMELINE

1908
Work begins on two new ships for the White Star Line, the *Titanic* and the *Olympic*.

1911, May 31st
The *Titanic* is launched.

1912
April 10th – The *Titanic* sets sail from Southampton and stops at Cherbourg, France.
April 11th – The *Titanic* calls at Queenstown, Ireland, then sets off across the Atlantic Ocean for New York.
April 14th, 11:40pm – The *Titanic* hits an iceberg.
• **Midnight** – The *Carpathia* hears the *Titanic*'s distress call and sets off to help.
April 15th, 12:10am – Passengers start getting into the *Titanic*'s lifeboats.
• **2:20am** – The *Titanic* sinks with the loss of around 1,500 lives.
• **3:30am** – The *Carpathia* arrives at the scene.
• **4:10am** – The *Carpathia* crew members find the lifeboats and begin to help the 705 survivors aboard.
• **9:00am** – The *Carpathia* sets off for New York.
April 18th, 9:30pm – The *Carpathia* docks in New York.

1953
People look for the wreck of the *Titanic* using sonar technology.

1985, September 1st
Robert Ballard discovers the wreck of the *Titanic* using the submersible *Argo*.

1998, August 10th
Scientists raise the Big Piece, a section of the *Titanic*'s hull, to the surface.

Acknowledgements

The publishers are grateful to the following organizations for their permission to reproduce material:

© **Corbis** back cover (Leonard de Selva), p1 (Ralph White), p11 (Ralph White), p13 (Leonard de Selva), p15 (Bettmann), pp16-17 (Hulton-Deutsch Collection), p21 (Underwood & Underwood), pp22-23 (Bettmann), p24 (Bettmann), p32 (Hulton-Deutsch Collection), p33 (Bettmann), p41 (Ralph White), p42 (POLAK MATTHEW/SYGMA), p44 bottom (Bettmann), p45 (Bettmann), p46 (Bettmann), p48 (Hulton-Deutsch Collection), p49 (Bettmann), p52 (Bettmann), p54 (Bettmann), p56 (PENNINGTON DONALD/SYGMA), p59 (Ralph White), p60 middle & bottom (Ralph White);
© **Getty Images** p34, p55 (*Titanic* ©1997 Twentieth Century Fox and Paramount Pictures Corporation. All rights reserved.), p62 (National Geographic);
© **Harland and Wolff Ltd.** p7, pp8-9, p12 bottom;
© **MARY EVANS PICTURE LIBRARY** p12 top, pp38-39, pp50-51; © **Mayfair Picture Library** p14;
© **popperfoto.com** pp18-19, p31, p44 top;
© **RMS Titanic, Inc.** p61.